CAMP SUMTER

The Pictorial History of Andersonville Prison

by
Ken Drew

(From a sketch made at the time by R.K. Sneden)

VIEW FROM THE OUTSIDE OF THE SOUTH GATE

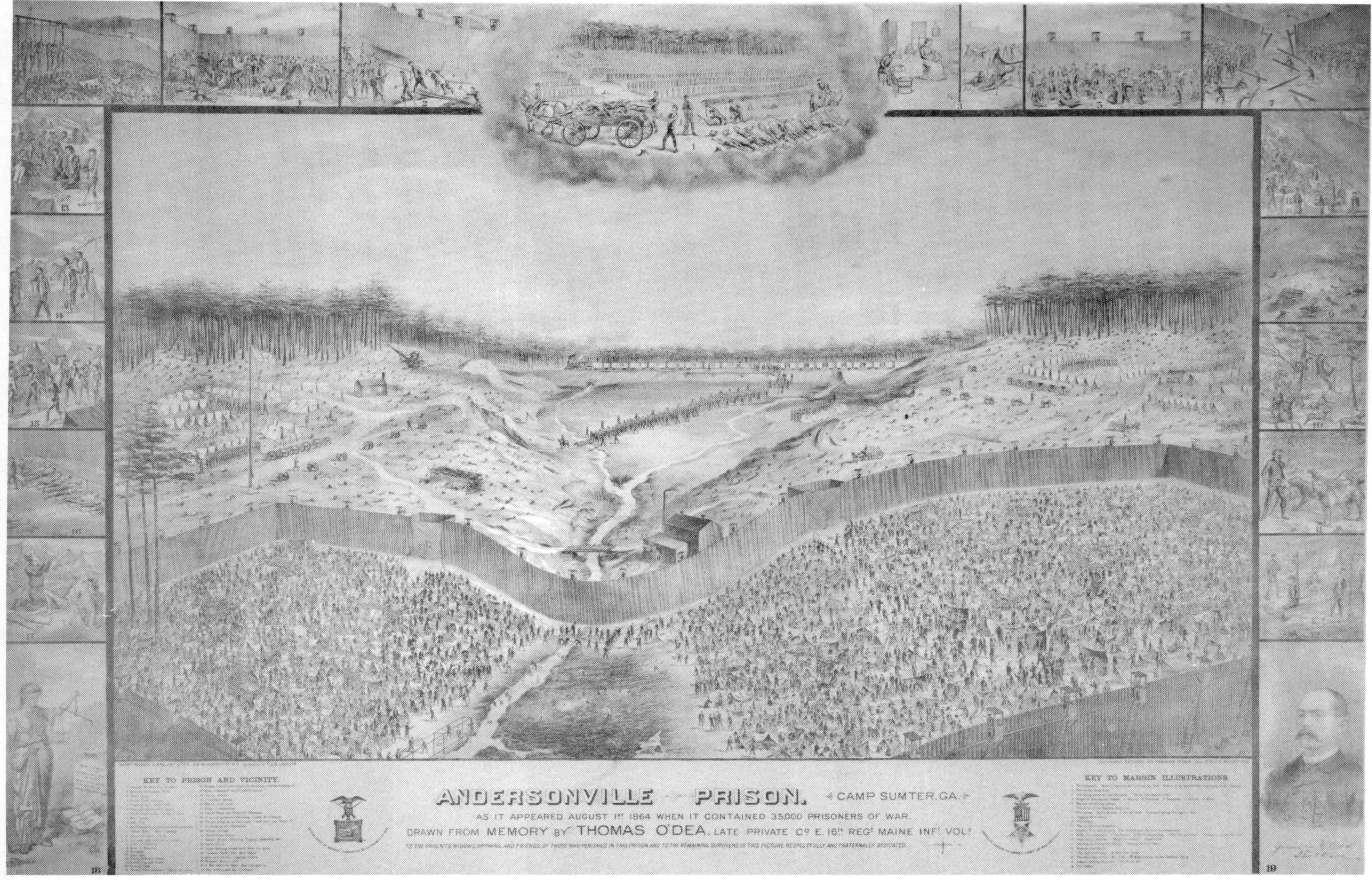

KEY TO PRISON AND VICINITY.
KEY TO MARGIN ILLUSTRATIONS
ANDERSONVILLE — PRISON. ◄CAMP SUMTER, GA.►
AS IT APPEARED AUGUST 1ST 1864 WHEN IT CONTAINED 35,000 PRISONERS OF WAR.
DRAWN FROM MEMORY BY THOMAS O'DEA, LATE PRIVATE CO. E. 16TH REGT MAINE INFT VOLS
TO THE PARENTS, WIDOWS, ORPHANS, AND FRIENDS OF THOSE WHO PERISHED IN THIS PRISON AND TO THE REMAINING SURVIVERS IS THIS PICTURE RESPECTFULLY AND FRATERNALLY DEDICATED.

This is an original photograph of the main road leading from the railroad depot in the city of Andersonville to the stockade. 50,000 Americans made this journey. For 13,000 prisoners and over a hundred guards, it was a one way trip.

Office of Captain Wirz as it looked when occupied.
Original Pen & Ink Sketch by Artist Marie Anderson.

STANTON HALTS PRISONER EXCHANGES

JULY 18, 1862:
Major General and Union Agent of Exchange John A. Dix, and Major General and Confederate Agent of Exchange Daniel H. Hill sign the Dix-Hill Cartel, authorizing the ready exchange of Northern and Southern military prisoners, a practice which has actually existed since the beginning battles of the war.

OCTOBER 27, 1863:
Charging that Confederate authorities have violated the Dix-Hill Cartel, as well as having mistreated captured Negro Union soldiers and their white officers, United States Secretary of War Edwin M. Stanton halts the exchange of prisoners of war, causing inmate populations on both sides to sharply increase.

OCTOBER 28, 1863:
General and Commander of the Confederate Army of Northern Virginia Robert E. Lee writes Confederate Secretary of War James A. Seddon, recommending that Union military prisoners held near Richmond, Virginia, be transferred to a facility in a state further south where food and supplies are more abundant.

NOVEMBER 24, 1863:
Confederate Secretary of War James A. Seddon orders Captain W. Sidney Winder to meet with Georgia Governor Joseph E. Brown at the state capitol in Milledgeville to choose a place in the Americus or Ft. Valley area for the establishment of a new Confederate prisoner of war camp.

DECEMBER 21, 1863:
Citing good natural resources and a close proximity to the railroad, Captain W. Sidney Winder orders construction of Camp Sumter Confederate Military Prison at the village of Andersonville in Sumter County, having purchased the land from local businessmen Benjamin B. Dykes and Wesley W. Turner.

FEBRUARY 3, 1864:
Captain and Camp Sumter Quartermaster Richard B. Winder writes Major and Columbus, Georgia, Commissary A.M. Allen, requesting that he send enough provisions to feed Andersonville, as the local supplier, Uriah B. Harrold, is able to supply only half of the needs of the post, adding that beef should be sent with the tallow attached for candlemaking.

FEBRUARY 7, 1864:
Brigadier General and Commander of Confederate Military Prisons John H. Winder, father of Captain and Post Commander W. Sidney Winder, and uncle of Captain and Post Quartermaster Richard B. Winder, notifies Camp Sumter that the first prisoners will arrive by way of Raleigh, North Carolina, and Columbia, South Carolina, accompanied by 61 guards.

FEBRUARY 17, 1864:
Captain and Quartermaster Richard B. Winder is startled by information received from the Confederate War Department that Union prisoners of war can no longer be fed in Richmond and are now on route to Camp Sumter, as the post is far from completed and supplies are unavailable in large amounts.

FEBRUARY 18, 1864:
Captain and Quartermaster Richard B. Winder is approached by several civilian employees on post complaining that they have not been paid in almost six weeks, Winder having earlier written Brigadier General and Commander of Military Prisons John H. Winder that 100 members of the guard force are without rifles.

FEBRUARY 19, 1864:
Captain and Quartermaster Richard B. Winder writes Albany, Georgia, Captain and Quartermaster C.H. Berry, and Captain and Commissary W.H. Brotherton, directing them to transfer corn arriving at Camp Sumter to Drew's Mill for processing into meal, and to take care that none of the supplies are lost on route to Andersonville.

PRISONERS ARRIVE FROM RICHMOND

FEBRUARY 20, 1864:

Captain and Quartermaster Richard B. Winder urgently requests Brigadier General and Commander of Confederate Military Prisons John H. Winder in Richmond, and Major and Florida Commissary P.W. White, to send beef and other rations in preparation for the arrival of the first prisoners.

FEBRUARY 23, 1864:

Desperately contacting Major and Florida Commissary P.W. White and suppliers in Georgia to send rations, Captain and Camp Sumter Quartermaster Richard B. Winder tries to procure offal from Captain and Albany Commissary W.H. Brotherton, but finds even slaughterhouse scraps difficult to obtain from the starving Confederacy.

FEBRUARY 25, 1864:

The first 500 Union prisoners arrive at Andersonville by rail from Richmond and are marched by Confederate guards one-half mile east of town to the barren and partially completed stockade, containing no shelter or sanitary facilities, only a three foot wide stream of water running through the prison.

FEBRUARY 27, 1864:

Chief Surgeon Isaiah H. White establishes a hospital two miles south of Andersonville to treat the scourge of smallpox, a contagious and deadly disease which arrived with the first prisoners on post, successfully utilizing many early experimental medical techniques to treat the illness, such as innoculations.

FEBRUARY 28, 1864:

Castle Reed, a small rectangular stockade at Camp Sumter located between the town of Andersonville and the main stockade, begins operations as a Union officers prison, and continues until May 7, 1864, when the 65 inmates are transferred to Camp Oglethorpe in Macon, Georgia.

Interior of Prison

PERSONS TAKES COMMAND

Post war photograph. Location of the South Gate.

FEBRUARY 29, 1864:
> Lieutenant Colonel Alexander W. Persons, a native of nearby Ft. Valley and commander of the Confederate 55th Georgia Infantry Regiment stationed as guards at Andersonville, takes charge of Camp Sumter, relieving Captain W. Sidney Winder who remains as an officer in various positions on post.

FEBRUARY 30, 1864:
> Captain and Quartermaster Richard B. Winder reports to Brigadier General and Commander of Military Prisons John H. Winder in Richmond that Camp Sumter is nearly completed and everything is working well, but locks, door fixtures, maintenance supplies, cooking implements, and a cook are still needed.

MARCH 2, 1864:
> Commander of Military Prisons John H..Winder complains to Confederate Secretary of War James A. Seddon that Lieutenant Colonel and Post Commander Alexander W. Persons does not keep him informed of events at Camp Sumter, Seddon later replying that if Winder does not like Persons, he should choose another commander.

MARCH 3, 1864:
> The stockade still unfinished and the post unable to buy heavy equipment, Captain and Quartermaster Richard B. Winder authorizes Sheriff W.B. Paul of Lee County to impress four mule driven wagons for use at Camp Sumter, preferably from a plantation which can afford the loss.

MARCH 4, 1864:
> The refusal of many local plantation owners to donate slave labor to Camp Sumter has prompted Lieutenant Colonel and Post Commander Alexander W. Persons to order that prisoners be recruited to finish building the post, and directs officers to provide enough men to bury the dead each day.

MARCH 15, 1864:
> Major and Columbus Commissary A.M. Allen writes Captain and Quartermaster Richard B. Winder that an officer has been assigned to serve as commissary at Camp Sumter, but first must have a storehouse to perform his duty, Winder later replying that Allen may either send the lumber to build or use space in a local church.

MARCH 16, 1864:

Lieutenant Colonel and Post Commander Alexander W. Persons orders troops and personnel at Camp Sumter to avoid speaking with the prisoners unless official business is transacted, and not to congregate on the loading platform at the Andersonville depot when trains are arriving or departing.

MARCH 20, 1864:

Under the direction of mechanic Samuel Heys, the 16½ acre, 15 foot high rectangular log stockade is completed, with guardposts called pigeon roosts at intervals along the top, and a low railing 15 feet inside running parallel to the walls called the deadline, which no prisoner may cross under penalty of being shot by a guard.

MARCH 27, 1864:

Captain Heinrich Hartman Wirz, native of Zurich, Switzerland, and combat veteran of the Confederate Fourth Battalion Louisiana Volunteer Infantry, severely wounded in the right shoulder at the Battle of Seven Pines, Virginia, takes charge as interior prison commandant, the officer directly in charge of the inmates.

MARCH 30, 1864:

Headquartered at Macon, General Howell Cobb takes command of the Reserve Corps of Georgia, the main guard force at Camp Sumter, consisting largely of boys under 17 years of age and men over 50; some so young, according to prisoner of war Sergeant Eugene Forbes, that they can barely see over the walls from the pigeon roosts.

MARCH 31, 1864:

Captain James W. Armstrong, Jr., takes charge as post commissary officer, relieving Captain and Quartermaster Richard B. Winder of the nearly impossible task of feeding 8,000 inmates and military personnel at Camp Sumter, a figure growing by the day, with ever decreasing rations.

APRIL 1, 1864:

Union military prisoners from several nations are now confined at Camp Sumter, along with residents of every state north and south, including Negroes and American Indians; Americus newspaper *Sumter Republican* reposting that many inside of the filthy stockade speak little or no English.

Castle Reed Stockade looking south. This was used as an officer's prison, located near the main stockade.

NO LUMBER FOR COFFINS

The Andersonville Prison Cemetery as it appeared shortly after the war.

APRIL 6, 1864:
Needy and ragged Camp Sumter inmates strip a dead prisoner of useful clothing before burial to discover that this unknown compatriot was a woman who had posed as a Union soldier, one of many in the war who, disguised as men, donned the blue or gray to fight for their country.

APRIL 11, 1864:
Captain and Quartermaster Richard B. Winder writes Major and Macon Quartermaster J.G. Michaeloffsky, asking why a load of lumber expected by rail from Macon 12 days ago has not arrived, threatening to report the matter to Confederate authorities in Richmond if the needed lumber is not sent to Andersonville immediately.

APRIL 14, 1864:
Captain and Quartermaster Richard B. Winder complains for a second time to Major and Macon Quartermaster J.G. Michaeloffsky that lumber must be sent as soon as possible, explaining that the lumber shortage is so great on post that necessary buildings cannot be constructed and the dead are being buried without coffins.

APRIL 24, 1864:
Confederate inspector Major Thomas P. Turner is quoted in the Georgia newspaper *Columbus Daily Enquirer* that an additional stockade should be built at Camp Sumter to relieve the prison overcrowding, and that the inmate hospital, now operating inside of the stockade, should be relocated elsewhere on post.

APRIL 26, 1864:
Chief Surgeon Isaiah H. White notifies Confederate Surgeon General Samuel P. Moore that 718 of the 2,697 patients in the prison hospital have died due to poor natural resources, a lack of supplies, the arrival of the first inmates before the prison was completed, and the location of the hospital within the stockade.

MAY 1, 1864:
The bakehouse, locate outside of the west wall near the prison creek, begins service, never preparing cooked rations for more than a fraction of the ever growing inmate population, while grease from the facility is discarded into the creek branch upstream of the stockade, polluting the only source of water for the prisoners.

CSA TOLD OF OVERCROWDING CONDITIONS

MAY 4, 1864:

Major General and Georgia Reserves Commander Howell Cobb inspects Camp Sumter and recommends that the stockade be enlarged and fortified, writing Confederate Adjutant General Samuel Cooper that no more prisoners should be sent to the already dangerously overcrowded prison.

MAY 5, 1864:

Major General and Georgia Reserves Commander Howell Cobb comments in a letter to Confederate Adjutant General Samuel Cooper that the stockade at Camp Sumter is packed to capacity with Union prisoners, adding that he hates to think what the death rate will be during the summer months if the present conditions remain.

MAY 6, 1864:

Camp Sumter Chief Surgeon Isaiah H. White recommends to Confederate inspector Captain Walter Bowie that the prison hospital be moved from the interior of the stockade, as it is situated near the unsanitary and polluted creek bed, where inmates attack sick prisoners and steal hospital equipment.

MAY 7, 1864:

The local newspaper *Sumter Republican* reports that Lieutenant Colonel and Post Commander Alexander W. Persons is performing his duties well, the deaths at Camp Sumter are due to regular camp diseases, and rations are adequate, but the bakehouse is inadequate to serve the present number of inmates.

MAY 8, 1864:

Captain and Camp Sumter Interior Prison Commandant Henry Wirz reports to Confederate authorities that the cramped and filthy stockade now holds 12,954 inmates and should be enlarged, adding that 728 prisoners have died, due in part to the location of the prison hospital inside of the stockade.

MAY 10, 1864:

Confederate Sergeant Edward C. Turner takes charge of the bloodhounds, one of the most controversial duties on post, due to accusations by some of the prisoners that the dogs not only track down but attack and maim escapees, under orders of Captain and Interior Prison Commandant Henry Wirz.

View of the stockade interior. Note man wearing suspenders at the lower left.

LOCAL CITIZENS FEAR ESCAPE

Stockade interior looking north along the stockade latrine.

MAY 13, 1864:

At a time that 18,000 inmates are guarded by 1,200 troops, Secretary of War James A. Seddon transfers several Confederate regiments from Camp Sumter to combat duty in Atlanta, aiding the Southern resistance against Union Major General William T. Sherman, but weakening the security of Andersonville.

MAY 14, 1864:

As a band from Macon plays, "The Girl I Left Behind Me," a farewell picnic is given by the prison staff and local citizens of Andersonville to honor the 26th Alabama Infantry Regiment, preparing to depart Camp Sumter for battle in North Georgia as ordered by the Confederate War Department.

MAY 20, 1864:

The newspaper *Sumter Republican* calls for Confederate reinforcements to secure the prison, as many local citizens fear that 20,000 prisoners will escape; the article also teasing Lieutenant Colonel and Post Commander Alexander W. Persons for his apparent relationship with an Americus woman.

MAY 22, 1864:

The inmate hospital, previously located inside of the disease ridden, filthy, and dangerous stockade, is relocated southeast of the prison in a shady oak grove, providing a healthier environment for the 1,250 patients, but doing little to lessen the high death rate caused by a lack of food and medicine.

MAY 23, 1864:

Major General and Georgia Reserves Commander Howell Cobb complains to Georgia Governor Joseph E. Brown that his policy of executive exemption from the military draft for all public officials in Georgia has caused a shortage of manpower in the Confederacy, especially at Camp Sumter.

MAY 25, 1864:

Captain and Interior Prison Commandant Henry Wirz posts a sign inside of the stockade stating that a group of inmates have planned a mass escape, threatening that if attempted, he will order the artillery, consisting partly of several Howitzer cannons loaded with canister shot, to open fire into the prison.

CAPTAIN WIRZ PROTESTS POOR RATIONS

MAY 26, 1864:

Confederate inspector Major Thomas P. Turner reports to Richmond that Captain and Interior Prison Commandant Henry Wirz is an efficient officer, but the polluted stockade creek at Camp Sumter is unfit for drinking and bathing, and the water current is of insufficient force to remove wastes from the feces laden creek bed.

JUNE 6, 1864:

Captain and Interior Prison Commandant Henry Wirz complains to Captain and Acting Post Adjutant R.D. Chapman that the cornmeal issued to the 24,000 prisoners and staff is unbolted; that is, ground with the husks and unfit for consumption, a factor partially responsible for the death rate of 100 per day later in the summer.

JUNE 15, 1864:

Camp Sumter Chief Surgeon Isaiah H. White appoints Union prisoner of war Private Dorance Atwater, Second New York Cavalry, to keep a register of the name, regiment, burial place, and date and cause of death of each inmate who dies at Camp Sumter, a document later known as the *Atwater Death List.*

JUNE 17, 1864:

Brigadier General and Confederate Commander of Military Prisons John H. Winder takes command of Camp Sumter, relieving Lieutenant Colonel Alexander W. Persons, who resumes command of the 55th Georgia Infantry Regiment stationed at Andersonville.

JUNE 18, 1864:

Brigadier General and Camp Sumter Post Commander John H. Winder writes Confederate General Braxton Bragg that sicknesses and furloughs have reduced the available guard force from 2,867 to 1,462, and recommends that reinforcements be sent to double that number.

JUNE 22, 1864:

Brigadier General and Post Commander John H. Winder orders Lieutenant S. Boyer Davis to hand deliver an urgent message to Major General and Georgia Reserves Commander Howell Cobb stating that the guard force at Camp Sumter must be reinforced and that no further prisoners should be sent to the overcrowded stockade.

Interior of the stockade. The creek at the east side looking northwest.

"RAIDERS" ARRESTED, PUT INTO STOCKS — TO BE TRIED

The graves of the Raiders. By request of prisoners, the six are buried separately from the others in the cemetery.

JUNE 23, 1864:
> Georgia Reserves Private James E. Anderson writes President Jefferson Davis that young guards in the pigeon roosts are shooting prisoners in the stockade who have not crossed the deadline, a point made earlier by Charles H. Thiot, another guard, in a letter to his wife.

JUNE 24, 1864:
> Brigadier General and Post Commander John H. Winder notifies Adjutant General Samuel Cooper that the prison is taxed to the utmost extent, the mortality rate is considerable, and more guards, surgeons, and engineers are needed; adding that any tents left at Belle Isle Prison in Richmond should be sent to Camp Sumter at once.

JUNE 25, 1864:
> Chief Surgeon Isaiah H. White establishes Camp Sumter Confederate Hospital to treat the sick troops on post, many of whom are dying from the same diseases as the prisoners, such as gangrene, scurvy, smallpox, and the biggest killer due in part to coarsely ground cornmeal, dysentery.

JUNE 26, 1864:
> One of 200 small businesses operating on Market Street inside of the stockade, including barbershops run by the prisoners, a sutler stand is erected by post employee James Selman to trade or sell such items as soap, tobacco, candy, and fresh vegetables to the inmates.

JUNE 29, 1864:
> The six ring leaders of the Raiders, a notorious band of renegade prisoners inside of the stockade who robbed and killed fellow inmates, are captured by a police force of prisoners called the Regulators, turned over to the Confederate authorities on post, and confined to the stocks until a trial can be arranged.

JULY 1, 1864:
> The inmate population have well exceeded the 12,000 man capacity for which the prison was designed, the stockade is enlarged from 16½ acres to 26½ acres extending north of the prison creek, Captain and Interior Prison Commandant Henry Wirz ordering half of the 26,000 inmates to immediately occupy the new section.

JULY 2, 1864:
> Georgia Governor Joseph E. Brown forwards a complaint from Andersonville townspeople to the Confederate War Department that 300 prisoners recently paroled by Brigadier General and Post Commander John H. Winder are roaming the town, trading with guards, and generally causing mischief.

WINDER APPROVES RAIDER EXECUTION

JULY 7, 1864:

Union prisoner Private Albert H. Shatzel strikes water from one of the 200 wells dug by inmates inside of the stockade during the prison's existence, producing sometimes fresh and sometimes brackish water, but supplementing the only other water source, the polluted prison creek.

JULY 8, 1864:

The 30,000 prisoners and staff receiving only one pound of cornmeal and bacon per man per day, inmates add to their meager diet with foods traded from guards or sutlers, and donations from local farms, such as fresh meat, rice, black beans, molasses, and chili peppers for the prevention of scurvy.

JULY 9, 1864:

Brigadier General and Post Commander John H. Winder sends a message to Confederate Adjutant General Samuel Cooper in Richmond desperately demanding reinforcements, claiming that the guard force at Camp Sumter is undisciplined, riddled with spies, threatening mutiny, and on the verge of desertion.

JULY 10, 1864:

Under approval of Camp Sumter Commander John H. Winder, the six ring leaders of the Raiders prison gang are tried within the stockade by a court of 24 Union sergeants organized by Captain and Interior Prison Commandant Henry Wirz, found guilty, and sentenced to hang, the minor gang members to be flogged by a gauntlet of inmates.

A closeup view of the prison population. Note the clothing, shebangs, and sutler's store.

Brigadier General John H. Winder, C.S.A.

Judge Robert Ould, Confederate Agent of Exchange

U.S. Secretary of War, E.M. Stanton

JULY 11, 1864:

Catholic chaplain Father Peter Whelan having administered last rights, the six Raider kingpins are hanged by fellow inmates inside of the stockade on gallows supplied by Captain and Interior Prison Commandant Henry Wirz, and by request of the other prisoners, buried dishonorably in a separate plot in the prison cemetery.

JULY 12, 1864:

Major General and Georgia Reserves Commander Howell Cobb writes his wife that many of the enlisted men are threatening desertion to coerce Brigadier General and Post Commander John H. Winder into issuing furloughs, a clear indication of the poor relationship which exists between Winder and the unruly Georgia Reserves.

JULY 14, 1864:

Camp Sumter surgeon W.J. Kerr reports to the nearby newspaper *Sumter Republican* that a baby has been born within the stockade to Mrs. H. Hunt, the wife of a prisoner, who, dressed as a man, remained with her husband through confinement and childbirth; Kerr adding that Mrs. Hunt and the child are now boarding with a local family.

JULY 18, 1864:

Captain and Quartermaster Richard B. Winder literally begs Confederate authorities for money to buy supplies for the inmates and pay the back salaries of the officers and enlisted men, stating in the letter to Major W. L. Bailey that the situation is desperate, as the post is completely without funds.

JULY 20, 1864:

Brigadier General and Post Commander John H. Winder reports that there are 2,421 Confederate officers and enlisted men on post; of these 517 are sick, 227 are on maintenance duty, and 126 are artillery men, leaving only 1,551 troops available to guard 29,000 Union prisoners.

JULY 25, 1864:

Brigadier General and Post Commander John H. Winder writes Adjutant General Samuel Cooper in Richmond that 20,000 prisoners should be moved immediately to other locations, and that there are 29,000 inmates, 2,650 troops, 500 white and Negro laborers, and not a ration on the post.

WINDER ORDERS STAR FORT BUILT

JULY 26, 1864:

A group of prisoners at Camp Sumter sends a petition to Governor John Brough of Ohio to ask that he intervene to break the stalemate between the South and North regarding prisoner exchanges, one of many such inmate petitions, some sent directly to President Lincoln, criticizing efforts taken by the United States to gain their release.

JULY 27, 1864:

Having learned of a planned attack on Camp Sumter by Union cavalry forces attached to Major General William T. Sherman, Commander John H. Winder orders Captain and Chief Engineer Theodore Moreno to construct Star Fort southwest of the stockade, as well as other earthwork fortifications at various points around the prison.

JULY 28, 1864:

Acting on recommendations from Confederate Generals Braxton Bragg, Howell Cobb, and John H. Winder, Secretary of War James A. Seddon orders that no more prisoners be sent to Camp Sumter, but prisoners captured at the Battle of Atlanta continue to fill the stockade, as there is no other military prison in the area.

JULY 29, 1864:

Convinced thaqt a Union raid on Andersonville is imminent, Brigadier General and Post Commander John H. Winder orders the artillery to open a cannonade of canister shot into the stockade if Federal troops attack the compound, and warns local counties that equipment and slaves will be taken to build fortifications if not donated.

JULY 30, 1864:

Major General George T. Stoneman, United States Cavalry, attempts a raid on Andersonville, but his force is seized near Macon by a local militia commanded by Major General Howell Cobb, and the captured enlisted men are sent to Camp Sumter, Stoneman becoming the highest ranking Union officer taken prisoner during the war.

JULY 31, 1864:

Under direction of Chief Surgeon Isaiah H. White, the inmate hospital is enlarged to accommodate 1,400 patients, improving conditions little, as 700 tents are still needed and 6,315 of the 30,000 prisoners are sick with scurvy, gangrene, and dysentery, along with 517 of the 2,700 Confederates on post.

AUGUST 1, 1864:

According to Captain and Interior Prison Commandant Henry Wirz, 83 escape tunnels have been found and filled to date, some more than 20 feet deep and 140 feed across; however, only one prisoner ever escaped using this method, most who attempted escape having done so by bribing or overpowering guards while on work detail.

Major General Howell Cobb, C.S.A.

James A. Seddon, Confederate Secretary of War

Dorance Atwater

A period print of the trial of Henry Wirz, October, 1865

17

*Washington
view of the C
Prison Cor
executed. Th
only known
Wirz is a pr
ney during
other photog
photo directl
around the r
right shows
gallows.*

ovember 10, 1865, within
ptain Henry Wirz, Interior
t of Camp Sumter, is
n the upper left corner is the
h of Wirz. To the right of
of Lewis Schade, his attor-
martial proceedings. The
ict the execution. Note the
— the noose is being placed
z. The picture directly to the
of Wirz dangling from the

19th Century work entitled, "Sunset At Andersonville."

U.S. REFUSES TO EXCHANGE PRISONERS

Stockade Interior looking north.

AUGUST 2, 1864:

Chief Surgeon Isaiah H. White complains to Brigadier General and Camp Sumter Commander John H. Winder that 21% of the 30,000 prisoners are sick, including 5,010 in the stockade and 1,305 in the hospital, scurvy is rampant due to scarce and unhealthy food, the commissary is without funds, and many inmates have no shelter.

AUGUST 4, 1864:

Confederate Surgeon General Samuel P. Moore writes Chief Surgeon Isaiah H. White that no further surgeons or supplies can be sent from the capital in Richmond to Camp Sumter, and blames White for not having anticipated the shortages at Andersonville and planned accordingly.

AUGUST 10, 1864:

Confederate Agent of Exchange Judge Robert Ould notifies Union authorities that the South will unilaterally release a number of prisoners of war from Camp Sumter if transportation is provided to take them home; however, two months will pass before the United States government acts on this proposal.

AUGUST 11, 1864:

Panic strikes as part of the west wall near the prison creek washes away during a storm, Brigadier General and Post Commander John H. Winder ordering the guards to man the gap to prevent the 33,000 inmates from escaping, and telegraphs Adjutant General Samuel Cooper in Richmond to send no more prisoners of war.

AUGUST 13, 1864:

A new source of fresh water for the prisoners gushes from the ground inside of the stockade near the recently washed away 100 foot portion of the west wall, saving hundreds of lives and believed by many to be an act of Divine Providence; thus the name given by the inmates, Providence Spring.

AUGUST 18, 1864:

Despite pleas from inmates at Camp Sumter to reestablish prisoner of war exchanges with the South, Union General in Chief Ulysses S. Grant refuses, claiming that released Confederates would join the resistance against the efforts of U.S. Major General William T. Sherman in Georgia.

AUGUST 19, 1864:

Colonels D.T. Chandler and R.H. Chilton of the Confederate Inspector General's office report that 15,000 prisoners should be transferred, and that the incompetence of Commissary J.W. Armstrong combined with a lack of supplies have driven the post to destitution, Chilton adding that these conditions are a reproach to the Confederacy.

AUGUST 20, 1864:

Post Commander John H. Winder responds to complaints from Georgia Governor Joseph E. Brown that paroled prisoners of war are roaming Andersonville disturbing the peace, writing Adjutant General Samuel Cooper that these inmates perform valuable duties on post, and the paroles relieve the harsh overcrowding within the stockade.

AUGUST 21, 1864:

Union Brigadier General T. Seymour, appointed by the United States War Department to investigate military prison conditions in the South, reports to Federal headquarters that the wisest course of action is to allow Union prisoners of war to remain confined at Andersonville, and not to initiate a prisoner exchange.

AUGUST 24, 1864:

Union Major General and Agent of Exchange Benjamin F. Butler informs Confederate Agent of Exchange Judge Robert Ould that the United States refuses to exchange Southern prisoners of war because of allegations that the Confederacy mistreats captured Negro soldiers, and refuses to include them in prisoner exchanges.

AUGUST 31, 1864:

Prisoner of war George W. Gray and guard Nazareth Allen observe that an inmate has died while confined in the stocks, a common means of military punishment at the time, but one, along with the chain gang, which will prompt murder charges against Captain and Camp Sumter Interior Prison Commandant Henry Wirz after the war.

SEPTEMBER 1, 1864:

R. Randolph Stevenson, surgeon at Camp Sumter, writes Surgeon General Samuel P. Moore that there are no buildings of any character to house the sick, and recommends that a special quartermaster be appointed with special authorization from Richmond to procure food, medicine, and supplies for Andersonville.

Post war photograph of the west wall taken from inside the stockade.

SECOND WALL BUILT AT PRISON — DEADLINE IS REMOVED

Post war view from inside the stockade looking northwest toward bakehouse.

SEPTEMBER 5, 1864:

Under orders of Adjutant General Samuel Cooper, the long awaited mass transfer of Union prisoners begins from Camp Sumter to Charleston and Florence, South Carolina, and Savannah and Millen, Georgia, reducing the inmate population at Andersonville from 33,000 to 5,000 by October.

SEPTEMBER 6, 1864:

Surgeon J. Crews Pelot reports to Surgeon E.D. Eland that conditions at Camp Sumter are generally deplorable, asking that the matter be given immediate attention, as the beds for the sick prisoners are without straw, the rations are inedible, and the hospitals on post are without medicine.

SEPTEMBER 12, 1864:

Confederate Surgeon General Samuel P. Moore directs Camp Sumter Chief Surgeon Isaiah H. White to assign members of the Andersonville medical staff to accompany the sick inmates as they are moved by train to the newly established prisoner of war camps in East Georgia and South Carolina.

SEPTEMBER 13, 1864:

Over 20 Union prisoners and Confederate guards are killed or wounded when a train transferring prisoners from Camp Sumter to Camp Lawton in Millen derails near the Andersonville depot, those inmates not wounded being returned to the stockade and relocated at a later date.

SEPTEMBER 15, 1864:

Improvements have recently been made to the compound, including a second stockade enclosing the first for security, barracks inside of the stockade on the north side, a better frame privy for the inmates on the fetid creek bed near the east wall, and the removal of the deadline until the middle of October.

SEPTEMBER 20, 1864:

Just prior to their departure for Camp Lawton Confederate Military Prison in Millen, a delegation of Union prisoners presents a gold watch to Lieutenant S.F. Mayes, 2nd Georgia Reserves, C.S.A., in appreciation for the kindness that he has shown them during their confinement at Camp Sumter.

DEATH RATE STANDS AT 23%

SEPTEMBER 24, 1864:
Captain Henry Wirz writes Brigadier General and Post Commander John H. Winder, rebutting a derogatory report of prison conditions made to Richmond by Confederate Colonel and Assistant Inspector General D.T. Chandler, and disclaiming charges that prison rations are not cooked and firewood is not provided for the inmates.

OCTOBER 8, 1865:
Brigadier General and Camp Sumter Commander John H. Winder, Captain and Quartermaster Richard B. Winder, and Chief Surgeon Isaiah H. White are transferred to Camp Lawton Confederate Military Prison in Millen, replaced by, respectively, Colonel George C. Gibbs, Captain J.H. Wright, and Dr. R. Randolph Stevenson.

OCTOBER 9, 1864:
Captain and Camp Sumter Quartermaster J.H. Wright directs the establishment of a factory for the manufacture of shoes for the inmates, as well as a brewery for the production of a medical drink called corn beer which combats scurvy, a major disease on post, caused by a diet lacking in fresh foods.

OCTOBER 18, 1864:
Major S.B. French of the Confederate Bureau of Substance notifies Colonel and Commissary General of Substance L.B. Northrop in Richmond that rations and supplies for the South, both for soldiers in the field, and inmates and staff of military prisons, are virtually depleted.

OCTOBER 19, 1864:
Dr. Joseph Jones, a Confederate pathologist assigned to Camp Sumter, reports to Surgeon General Samuel P. Moore that the 23% death rate at Andersonville is due to dysentery, scurvy, and gangrene, caused in large part by poor rations, little medicine, and the accumulation of feces within the stockade.

Postwar photo shows north end of the stockade wall looking south.

The Steamer Sultana

OCTOBER 29, 1864:

Brigadier General John H. Winder having complained to Richmond that several officers of the First Georgia Reserves are committing acts of disorderly conduct at Camp Sumter, Major General and Georgia Reserves Commander Howell Cobb responds that if these allegations are true, Winder should have come to him first.

NOVEMBER 12, 1864:

Captain and Interior Prison Commandant Henry Wirz notifies Captain and Assistant Quartermaster T.W. Neely that a shipment of goods for the inmates has arrived on post, consisting of 399 blankets, 60 pairs of shoes, 240 pairs of pants, 396 pairs of drawers, 396 pairs of sox, and 324 shirts.

NOVEMBER 22, 1864:

The prisoner of war population standing at 1,500 with escapes and desertions occuring regularly, Major and Assistant Adjutant General W. Carver Hall comments in a letter to his office in Richmond that while recently visiting Andersonville, he saw the inmates scavenging and digging for roots inside the stockade.

DECEMBER 24, 1864:

3,500 Union prisoners of war previously transferred from Camp Sumter to Camp Lawton, then to another military prison in Thomasville, are returned to Andersonville by order of Confederate General Pierre G.T. Beauregard, because Millen and Thomasville are no longer secure from Union cavalry raids.

SCANDAL ROCKS CAMP SUMTER

DECEMBER 27, 1864:

Scandal rocks Camp Sumter when Dr. H.H. Clayton, who recently replaced Chief Surgeon R. Randolph Stevenson, discovers that $100,000.00 is missing from the medical supply fund and calls in Confederate investigators, but the war will end before Stevenson can be brought to trial on embezzlement charges.

JANUARY 1, 1865:

A group of officers at Camp Sumter, including Captain and Interior Prison Commandant Henry Wirz, sends a resolution to several Southern newspapers stating that Dr. R. Randolph Stevenson was an effective, talented, and capable chief surgeon while serving at Andersonville.

JANUARY 15, 1865:

Captain and Interior prison Commandant Henry Wirz issues a memorandum regarding a woman named Ann Williams who has arrived at Camp Sumter to aid the prisoners, stating that Williams is offering sexual intercourse to the inmates, but not as a prostitute, as she does not charge for services rendered.

JANUARY 24, 1865:

Adjutant General Samuel Cooper orders Brigadier General and Confederate Commander of Prisons John H. Winder, presently at his headquarters in Columbia, South Carolina, to release all prisoners held in irons or close confinement, as Federal authorities have notified Richmond that Northern prisons are doing the same.

JANUARY 25, 1865:

Commander of Confederate Military Prisons John H. Winder writes Adjutant General Samuel Cooper that the prisons are overstaffed with guards and to send no more troops, adding that prisons should not be placed at the same location as military installations because of conflicts which arise between the commanders of both facilities.

Living along the deadline, 1864

PRISONER EXCHANGES RESUME

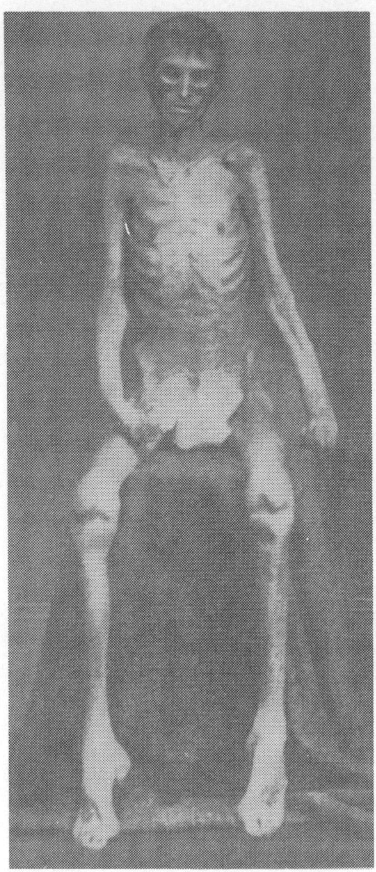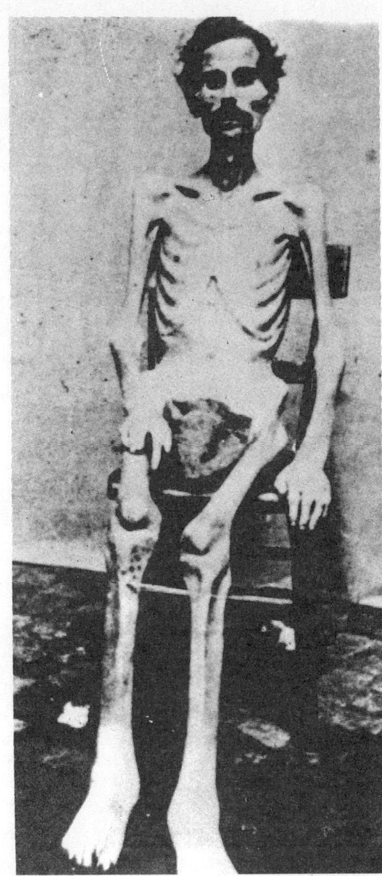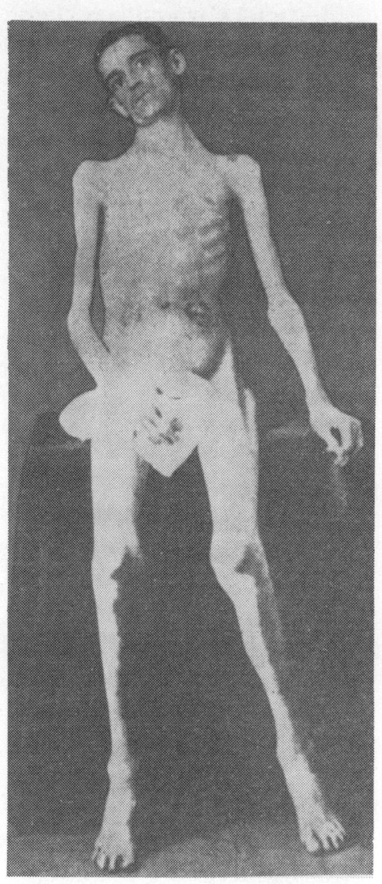

Victims of the conditions of Southern prisons. Such extreme cases of malnutrition and scurvy existed in Northern prisons as well.

FEBRUARY 6, 1865:

Brigadier General John H. Winder dies of a heart attack and is succeeded by Major General Gideon J. Pillow as Commander of Confederate Military Prisons, leaving Captain and Interior Prison Commandant Henry Wirz, Winder's former second in command at Camp Sumter, to face murder charges after the war.

FEBRUARY 26, 1865:

Captain and Interior Prison Commandant Henry Wirz writes Acting Assistant Adjutant General G.W. McPhail that many of the paroled prisoners who are performing valuable duties on post have no shoes, and requests permission to purchase either shoes or the leather to construct them, as many of the inmates are cobblers by trade.

MARCH 15, 1865:

In accordance with an agreement between Union General-in-Chief Ulysses S. Grant and Confederate Agent of Exhange Judge Robert Ould, prisoner exchanges resume with Captain Henry Wirz immediately paroling Camp Sumter prisoners for exchange at the agreed location of Big Black Bridge in Mississippi.

APRIL 5, 1865:

Colonel and Camp Sumter Commander George C. Gibbs notifies Assistant Adjutant General W. Sidney Winder that all of the inmates will soon be removed from the prison, except for 20 too sick to travel, and transferred to Union headquarters in Jacksonville, Florida, for exchange with Federal authorities.

LOCAL CITIZENS SEIZE CAMP WAREHOUSE

APRIL 17, 1865:

Brigadier General and Union Commander of Jacksonville E.P. Scammon, having previously agreed to exchange prisoners, today stops 2,500 Camp Sumter inmates on route to Jacksonville and directs them to return to Andersonville, under orders of U.S. Major General Quincy A. Gillmore, who kills the exchange.

APRIL 18, 1865:

General in Chief Robert E. Lee having surrendered nine days earlier, Union Major General William T. Sherman accepts the initial surrender of Confederate General Joseph E. Johnston and offers a parole to those under his command, a condition under which Henry Wirz will later claim to be covered, and therefore, immune from prosecution.

APRIL 26, 1865:

In Virginia, actor John Wilkes Booth, who assassinated President Abraham Lincoln 12 days earlier at Ford's Theatre in Washington, D.C., is cornered by United States troops in the barn of Richard H. Garrett and shot to death, reportedly by Boston Corbett, a former Union prisoner of war at Camp Sumter.

APRIL 27, 1865:

The streamer Sultana, packed with 2,000 recently released Camp Sumter prisoners headed north for home, catches fire after an accidental boiler explosion and sinks into the Mississippi River near Memphis, Tennessee, killing 1,400 passengers and becoming the deadliest ship disaster in American history.

APRIL 28, 1865:

Among the few remaining prisoners of war too sick to be exchanged, the last of the 12,912 inmates to die at Camp Sumter is buried in the congested prison cemetery one-half mile north of the stockade, the first having been laid to rest two days after the arrival of the first prisoners, February 17, 1864.

MAY 4, 1865:

Colonel and Post Commander George C. Gibbs releases the last prisoner held at Camp Sumter to Union authorities in Baldwin, Florida, and returns to Andersonville to find the quartermaster storehouse has been looted by a force of guards and local townspeople, many of whom are impoverished due to the war.

Interior of stockade looking north, showing deadline.

CLARA BARTON ARRIVES TO IDENTIFY GRAVES

Henry Wirz (An artist's conception)

The office of Captain Wirz, located in the town of Andersonville

MAY 5, 1865:

Former Andersonville Captain and Quartermaster Richard B. Winder informs his attorney George T. Garrison that all personal property related to Camp Sumter has been surrendered to Federal authorities, except for a few watches belonging to Andersonville prisoners, as he does not know to whom each item belongs.

MAY 7, 1865:

Under protest, claiming that he is exempt from prosecution under the surrender terms signed by Generals Sherman and Johnston, Interior Prison Commandant Henry Wirz is arrested at Andersonville by U.S. Captain N.E. Noyes under orders of Major General James H. Wilson, on charges of murdering Union prisoners of war.

MAY 8, 1865:

Henry Wirz, former Camp Sumter Interior Prison Commandant, writes U.S. Major General James H. Wilson that he is innocent of all charges of mistreating prisoners, and states that as soon as possible he intends to return to Europe with his family, asking that they be protected by Federal authorities until then.

MAY 12, 1865:

In an attempt to avoid prosecution, former Camp Sumter Commander George C. Gibbs writes U.S. General E.M. McCook that Henry Wirz, not he, was in charge of the prisoners; Gibbs adding that he never had direct contact with the inmates, nor had one ever complained to him of the conditions inside of the stockade.

MAY 31, 1865:

U.S. Assistant Adjutant General E.D. Townsend directs Major General C.C. Augur to take charge of former interior prison commandant Henry Wirz, and place the prisoner under secure confinement in the Old Capitol Prison in Washington, D.C., until a court martial can be arranged.

JUNE 1, 1865:

U.S. Major General James H. Wilson appoints W.A. Griffith to be the first superintendent of the prison cemetery at Andersonville, responsible for assisting in the proper placement of the headstones, and maintaining and repairing the graves, some in such poor condition that human remains are exposed.

JULY 25, 1865:

An expedition sent by U.S. Secretary of War Edwin M. Stanton arrives at Andersonville to assist Superintendent W.A. Griffith in the preservation, enclosure, and marking of the graves in the prison cemetery, the group including Clara Barton, founder of the American Red Cross, and former inmate Dorance Atwater.

WIRZ MAINTAINS HIS INNOCENCE

AUGUST 23, 1865:

Henry Wirz is brought to trial before the Special Military Commission, a panel of high ranking U.S. Army officers called by President Andrew Johnson and headed by Major General Lew Wallace, on charges of murdering and conspiring to murder prisoners of war under his care at Camp Sumter.

AUGUST 27, 1865:

Henry Wirz, on trial in Washington, D.C., writes the newspaper *New York News*, asking for assistance regarding his current legal problems, claiming that he was never cruel to a prisoner while interior prison commandant at Camp Sumter, and that the deadly conditions within the stockade were beyond his control.

AUGUST 30, 1865:

Former Camp Sumter quartermaster Richard B. Winder, now jailed in chains, writes Major N. Church at Accomac Court House, Virginia, that he had not been inside of the stockade more than six times during the existence of the prison, and never had any direct contact with the prisoners, except those on parole who he treated well.

SEPTEMBER 1, 1865:

Almost all major Confederate figures from Camp Sumter and Camp Lawton military prisons, including quartermaster Richard B. Winder, and chief surgeons Isaiah H. White and R. Randolph Stevenson, are now serving various jail terms on charges of conspiring with Henry Wirz to murder prisoners of war.

SEPTEMBER 11, 1865:

Captain Samuel Gillmore arrests and incarcerates George T. Garrison, attorney for jailed Camp Sumter quartermaster Richard B. Winder, for possessing 34 pocket watches belonging to Union prisoners, and turns both Garrison and the watches over to Brigadier General L.C. Baker.

SEPTEMBER 12, 1865:

Former Confederate Vice President Alexander H. Stephens has written a Mrs. McVeigh of Boston, Massachusetts, stating that he never had any association with Camp Sumter except to protest the poor prison conditions there, the letter having fallen into the hands of U.S. Secretary of War Edwin M. Stanton.

The train depot in the town of Andersonville, 1864

Boston Corbett, a former Andersonville prisoner.
He is credited with having killed John Wilkes Booth.

An artist's conception of a prisoner shot at the deadline.

SEPTEMBER 20, 1865:
> Andersonville area native Ambrose Spencer testifies at the trial of Henry Wirz, stating that plenty of food was available in the vicinity of Camp Sumter, but Wirz refused to allow local produce to be fed to the inmates, a contrast to the defense position that provisions were unattainable.

SEPTEMBER 21, 1865:
> The newspaper *Sumter Republican* reports that testimony has been submitted in the trial of Henry Wirz, alledging that Camp Sumter commander John H. Winder and interior prison commandant Wirz prevented a group of local women from delivering a load of food to the prisoners, and cursed them for having made the effort.

SEPTEMBER 22, 1865:
> At the Wirz trial in Washington, D.C., Phillip Cashmeyer, employee of the Confederate government who knew Henry Wirz when he was stationed as a prison commandant in Richmond, testifies that Wirz was a cruel and profane man who implemented strict discipline upon the Union prisoners who were held there.

SEPTEMBER 26, 1865:
> Resulting from a squabble concerning the publication of the *Atwater Death List* from Camp Sumter, Army authorities jail Dorance Atwater, the Union prisoner who kept the register of the inmates buried in the cemetery, but releases him two months later under an amnesty granted by President Andrew Johnson.

OCTOBER 11, 1865:
> James Duncan, a former sutler at Camp Sumter and defense witness in the trial of Henry Wirz, is arrested in open court on charges of conspiring with Wirz to commit acts of cruelty to prisoners, one of several witnesses who are denied the opportunity to testify in the case.

OCTOBER 19, 1865:

Felix de la Baume, a self-proclaimed Union prisoner of war and grandnephew of Marquis de Lafayette, and one of the many chief witnesses for the prosecution in the trial of Henry Wirz, is hired as a clerk by the U.S. Department of the Interior on the same day that he presents the most damaging testimony against Wirz.

OCTOBER 21, 1865:

Running a front page story of the Henry Wirz trial, the New York Newspaper *Harper's Weekly* reports that the health of Wirz is so poor that he must recline in the courtroom on a sofa, adding that the preponderance of evidence and testimony points to the certain guilt of the defendant.

OCTOBER 22, 1865:

Judge Advocate Colonel N.P. Chipman introduces evidence and testimony to the Special Military Commission trying Henry Wirz concerning the killing of prisoners, presenting former Andersonville inmates who swear under oath that they saw Wirz commit murder and order others to do so.

OCTOBER 24, 1865:

The nationally reported and precedent setting trial of Henry Wirz concludes, with court physicians C.M. Ford and John C. Bates testifying that Wirz is so ill with scurvy that his arms and legs are virtually incapacitated, disputing previous testimony from former inmates that as interior prison commandant, Wirz shot, beat, and kicked Union prisoners.

OCTOBER 26, 1865:

Convinced that a guilty verdict is forthcoming, Louis Schade, attorney for Henry Wirz, urges President Andrew Johnson not to execute his client, charging in the letter that the trial was improperly conducted, as the Special Military Commission appointed by Johnson either ignored or excluded testimony which would have cleared Wirz.

OCTOBER 31, 1865:

Judge Advocate General J. Holt announces the verdict of the Special Military Commission trying Henry Wirz, finding the former Confederate officer guilty of murdering and conspiring to murder Union prisoners, and sentences Wirz to death by hanging, the results immediately forwarded to President Andrew Johnson for approval.

President Andrew Johnson, U.S.A.

The Press Corps that covered Henry Wirz' trial

WIRZ NOTIFIED OF HIS EXECUTION

S.P. Moore, Surgeon General, C.S.A.

Clara Barton

NOVEMBER 6, 1865:

Upon notification that the Special Military Commission has sentenced him to death, Henry Wirz writes President Andrew Johnson asking for either an executive pardon or an immediate execution, explaining that he is weary of prison and wishes to be granted liberty or death.

NOVEMBER 8, 1865:

Consul General of Switzerland John Hitz, and Estwick Evans, a private citizen who supported the Union in the war, add their names to those calling for a presidential reprieve of the death sentence of Henry Wirz, many claiming that Wirz is simply the focus of Northern revenge against the South.

NOVEMBER 9, 1865:

Following the refusal of President Andrew Johnson to halt the execution of Henry Wirz as requested earlier in the day by attorney Louis Schade, Wirz writes Schade thanking him for handling the case, and asks that Schade and the people of the South care for his penniless family after his death.

NOVEMBER 10, 1865:

Proclaiming innocence to the end, telling the officer conducting the execution that he was only obeying orders as interior prison commandant at Camp Sumter, Heinrich Hartman Wirz is hanged near the U.S. Capitol at 10:32 a.m., dying slowly to the concerted voice of Union soldiers chanting, "Remember Andersonville."

NOVEMBER 11, 1865:

Major General C.C. Auger reports to U.S. Assistant Adjutant General E.D. Townsend that Henry Wirz has been executed and interred at the Arsenal Grounds near Washington, D.C., next to the grave of one of the recently executed Lincoln assassination conspirators, George Atzerodt.

NOVEMBER 21, 1865:

Felix de la Baume, a major prosecution witness in the Henry Wirz trial and self-proclaimed survivor of Andersonville prison, is discovered to be Felix Oeser, a Union deserter who concocted his entire testimony, and is fired from his job at the U.S. Department of the Interior, eleven days after the execution of Wirz.

FEBRUARY 1, 1866:

The newspaper *New York Tribune* publishes the *Atwater Death List* from Camp Sumter, following months of bureaucratic wrangling between Dorance Atwater, aided by Clara Barton, who demanded publication of the Union fatalities for the next of kin, and the United States government which refused.

PEACE RETURNS TO ANDERSONVILLE

NOVEMBER 12, 1867:

The United States Congress takes retribution for the "war crimes at Andersonville" by harshly and ratically reconstructing the former Confederate states, having earlier called former Confederate General in Chief Robert E. Lee to answer erroneous charges of conspiring to injure Union prisoners of war.

MAY 21, 1868:

Post-war Andersonville now consists of a few buildings in the provincial village, which survives largely unchanged from pre-war years, the fast deteriorating, once infamous stockade and post, and what will for over a hundred years be one of the most visited sites in Georgia, Andersonville National Cemetery.

The Henry Wirz Trial, Harper's Weekly, October 21, 1865.

BODY OF WIRZ MUTILATED BEFORE BURIAL

Burying the dead in mass graves without coffins.

FEBRUARY 26, 1869:

Having finally obtained the remains of Henry Wirz from Federal authorities for proper burial, attorney Louis Schade finds that various body parts have been removed and displayed for public viewing at the Old Capitol Prison, and demands that body United States government return the entire corpse to the Wirz family.

MARCH 2, 1869:

With Reverend Father Boyle, a chaplain from Camp Sumter, conducting the service, and family members and close friends, including Louis Schade, attending, Henry Wirz, the Swiss immigrant who became the most controversial soldier in America's most controversial war, is laid to rest at Mount Olivet Cemetery near Washington, D.C.

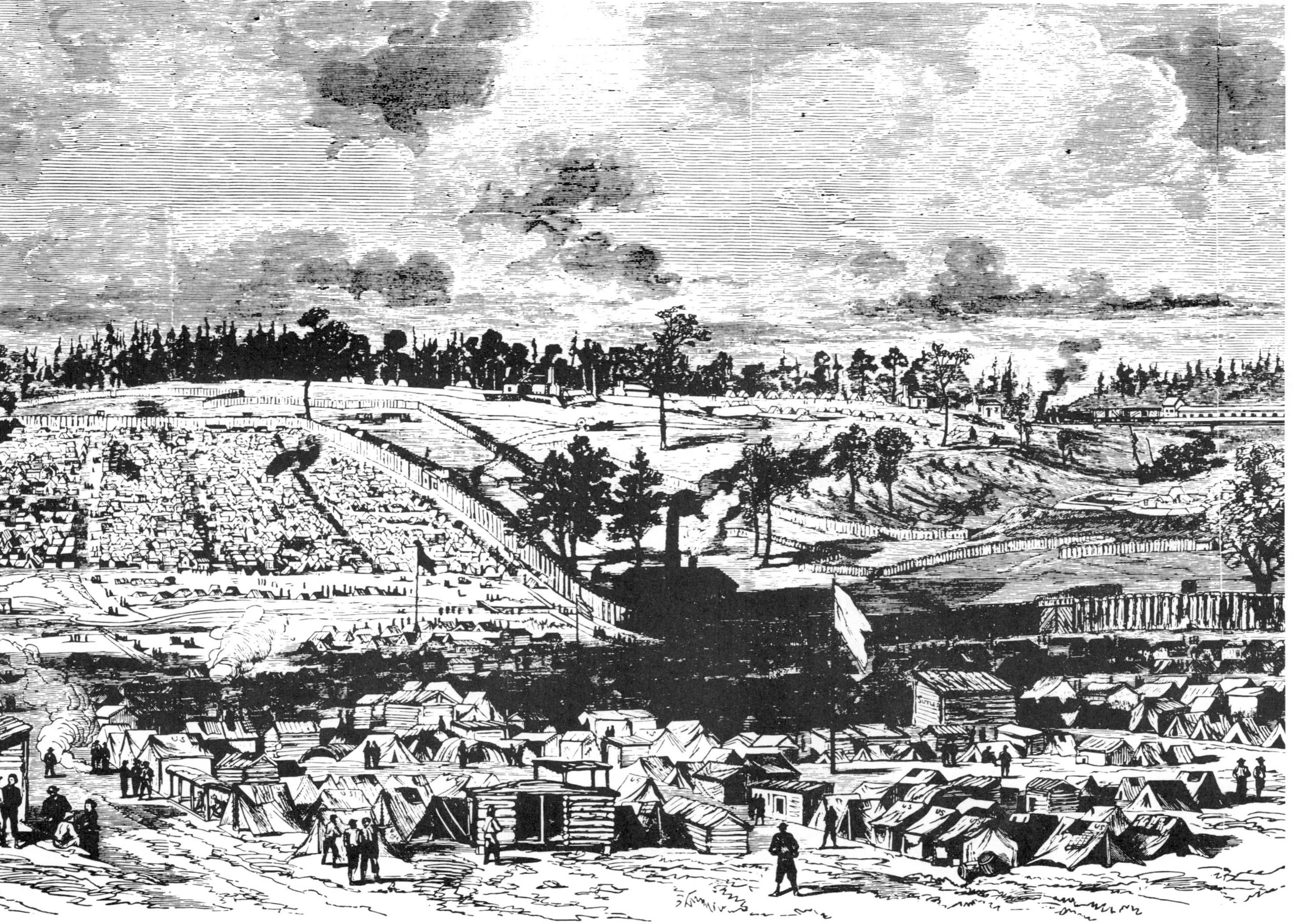

PRISON PEN AT ANDERSONVILLE, GA.—FROM A DRAWING BY R. SNEDEN, OF THE TOPOGRAPHICAL ENGINEER CORPS. July 2d, 1864.